T0401489

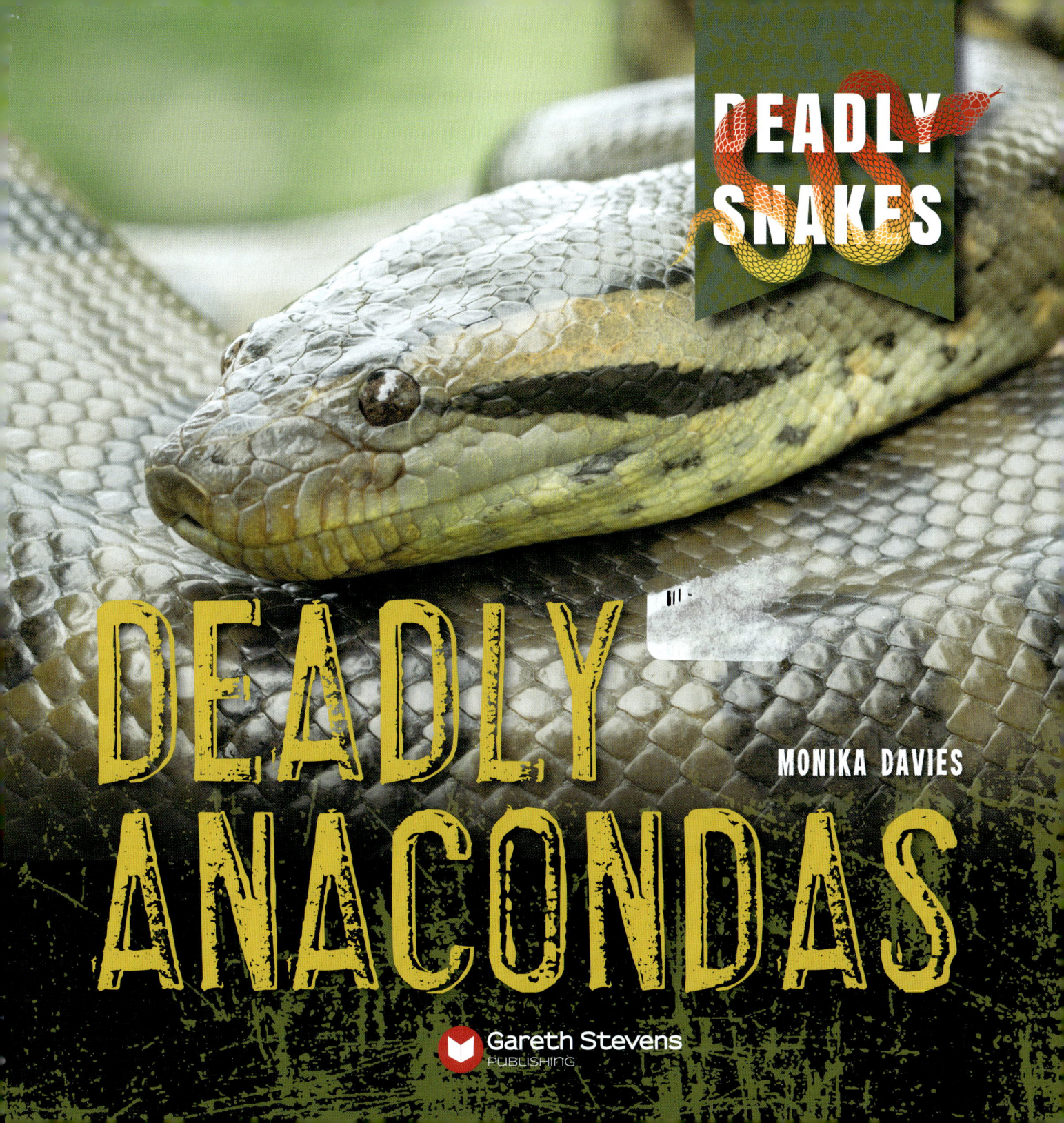

DEADLY SNAKES

DEADLY ANACONDAS

MONIKA DAVIES

Gareth Stevens
PUBLISHING

Please visit our website, www.garethstevens.com. For a free color catalog of all our high-quality books, call toll free 1-800-542-2595 or fax 1-877-542-2596.

Library of Congress Cataloging-in-Publication Data
Names: Davies, Monika, author.
Title: Deadly anacondas / Monika Davies.
Description: New York : Gareth Stevens Publishing, [2023] | Series: Deadly snakes | Includes index.
Identifiers: LCCN 2021050757 (print) | LCCN 2021050758 (ebook) | ISBN 9781538279724 (set) | ISBN 9781538279731 (library binding) | ISBN 9781538279717 (paperback) | ISBN 9781538279748 (ebook)
Subjects: LCSH: Anaconda–Juvenile literature. | Poisonous snakes–Juvenile literature.
Classification: LCC QL666.O63 D38 2023 (print) | LCC QL666.O63 (ebook) | DDC 597.96/7–dc23/eng/20211201
LC record available at https://lccn.loc.gov/2021050757
LC ebook record available at https://lccn.loc.gov/2021050758

First Edition

Portions of this work were originally authored by Sebastian Avery and published as *Anacondas*. All new material this edition authored by Monika Davies.

Published in 2023 by
Gareth Stevens Publishing
29 E. 21st Street
New York, NY 10010

Designer: Sheryl Kober
Editor: Monika Davies

Photo credits: Cover, p. 1 Mark_Kostich/Shutterstock.com; cover (snake illustration) vinap/Shutterstock.com; cover, pp. 1–24 (background texture) Anna Timoshenko/Shutterstock.com; pp. 1–24 (snakeskin) Natalliya85/Shutterstock.com; pp. 1–24 (halftone texture) MPFphotography/Shutterstock.com; pp. 3, 8, 19 (snake illustration) vinap/Shutterstock.com; pp. 4, 7, 11, 12, 16, 20 (fatal facts texture) Pakhnyushchy/Shutterstock.com; p. 5 wayak/Shutterstock.com; p. 6 JR_photo /Shutterstock.com; p. 9 PUMPZA/Shutterstock.com; p. 10 Yevgen Kravchenko/Shutterstock.com; p. 13 SachinSubran/Shutterstock.com; p. 14 Milan1983/Shutterstock.com; p. 15 chrisbrignell/Shutterstock.com; p. 17 tome213/Shutterstock.com; p. 18 chamleunejai/Shutterstock.com; p. 21 Vadim Petrakov/Shutterstock.com;

Printed in the United States of America

CPSIA compliance information: Batch #CSGS23: For further information contact Gareth Stevens, New York, New York, at 1-800-542-2595.

Find us on

CONTENTS

Words in the glossary appear in **bold** type the first time they are used in the text.

THE ALARMING ANACONDA

In **tropical** South America, a deadly snake swims in streams and **swamps**. This snake watches and waits for its next meal. When a large animal comes to the water for a drink, this snake strikes quickly!

Meet the anaconda, one of the world's largest snakes. The anaconda is a lethal, or deadly, predator. It's large and strong enough to kill deer, wild pigs, and even jaguars! This snake has surprising strength and can **strangle** large prey, or the animals it hunts for food.

FATAL FACTS

There are four species, or kinds, of anacondas, including the Beni or Bolivian anaconda, the yellow or Paraguayan anaconda, the dark-spotted anaconda, and the green anaconda, the largest of them all. This book focuses on the green anaconda.

All snakes are carnivores, or meat eaters, including green anacondas.

Adult female anacondas don't have many predators because they're so large! But male anacondas are smaller and need to keep themselves safe from more predators.

GREEN GIANTS

Named for the color of its skin, the green anaconda can be green, grayish green, or brownish green. Most also have black spots. These colors allow the anaconda to hide from prey in its jungle surroundings.

As the heaviest snake in the world, the green anaconda can grow up to 30 feet (9.1 m) long and weigh more than 550 pounds (250 kg)! The anaconda's size helps it catch many kinds of prey, including birds, fish, and even big cats.

FATAL FACTS

The green anaconda is an **apex** predator. Anacondas eat a lot of different prey, but they only have a few predators. The green anaconda's large size makes it hard to kill and eat.

GROWING UP

While some snakes lay eggs, others—like the green anaconda—give birth to live young. Mother anacondas often give birth to 20 to 40 live young at one time. Larger snakes can have as many as 80 babies. The mother leaves her babies as soon as they're born. Anaconda babies are about 2 feet (0.6 m) long, and they quickly learn to hide and hunt.

Baby anacondas grow rather quickly for three to four years. By that time, they have become skilled hunters. They're also ready to start having babies.

By the time a green anaconda is around three years old, it may be nearly 10 feet (3 m) long.

WHERE ANACONDAS LIVE

LLANOS GRASSLANDS

ORINOCO RIVER

Venezuela

Colombia

AREAS WHERE
ANACONDAS LIVE

AMAZON RIVER

SOUTH AMERICA

Brazil

Green anacondas live in the northern part of South America. Most live near the Orinoco River in Colombia, the Amazon River in Brazil, and in the Llanos grasslands in Venezuela.

NATURAL SWIMMERS

Anacondas live in South American rain forests and wetlands where there is a lot of water. Green anacondas are rather slow and clumsy on land, but in the water, they're expert swimmers.

Anacondas like to rest on logs near water. This allows them to warm up in the sun. They may also hide in slow-moving streams. There, they can cool off. Everything but their eyes and **nostrils** may be below water, making it very hard for prey to see them hiding.

FATAL FACTS

The scientific name for the green anaconda is *Eunectes murinus*. This is a combination of the Greek word for "good swimmer" and the Latin word for "mouse colored."

PATIENT PREDATORS

Anacondas are patient animals. They spend a lot of time lying around, waiting for food. They often hide in **shallow** water or even mud. Anacondas usually hunt by ambushing their prey. That means they hide and wait for animals to wander by—and then they strike! They may hang in branches above rivers, which allows them to drop into the water and surprise prey.

Anacondas are most active in early evening and at night when it's cooler. They may travel to find food or to find a **mate**.

FATAL FACTS

Anacondas belong to a group of snakes called constrictors. These snakes don't use **venom** to kill prey. They kill by squeezing prey to death!

During the dark of the night, the anaconda can hide more easily and surprise its prey.

Anacondas usually hunt alone in their home area. They come together with other anacondas only during mating season.

HUNTING SENSES

An anaconda has eyes and nostrils on top of its head. This allows the anaconda to hide almost completely underwater while waiting for its next meal. The anaconda can use its forked tongue to pick up scents around it. It also senses **vibrations** from nearby animals.

The anaconda has small pits on its upper lip. These pits help it sense body heat from other animals. All these senses make the anaconda a successful hunter. Their senses help them find and catch prey.

WHAT'S FOR DINNER?

Anacondas eat a wide range of animals. They aren't picky eaters! They eat smaller animals such as fish, birds, turtles, and other snakes. They also catch and eat larger rain forest animals such as deer, caimans, capybaras, peccaries, tapirs, and jaguars.

Anacondas are sometimes known to eat pets and livestock. They rarely attack people, but there are a few reports of this. People don't often go into the anacondas' home range, and anacondas like to remain in their wet **habitats**.

FATAL FACTS

Anacondas are also cannibals! That means they'll eat their own kind. Female anacondas sometimes will eat smaller male anacondas.

Green anacondas only need to eat one large meal every few weeks. They **digest** their food slowly.

An anaconda's jaw is made of bones that are connected to the skull by stretchy pieces of tissue. This allows an anaconda to swallow prey that's much bigger than itself!

TIME TO EAT

The anaconda stays hidden until its prey is within reach. When a prey animal comes close, the snake strikes. It grabs the prey with its sharp **fangs** and hangs on tight. As the prey struggles, the anaconda wraps its long, strong body around it and squeezes. The squeezing cuts off the prey's blood and air supply, and it dies quickly.

Once the prey is dead, the anaconda stretches its jaw and opens its mouth really wide. It eats the prey head first—and in one big gulp!

CARING FOR THE ANACONDA

While anacondas are deadly predators, they do have predators of their own. Humans are the greatest danger to these large snakes. People sometimes hunt anacondas for their skin or to sell them as pets.

Right now, anacondas are not an **endangered** species. Still, green anacondas mainly live in tropical rain forests. In the last 50 years, people have cut down around 17 percent of the Amazon rain forest. Caring for the anaconda means caring for its home. Anacondas may be deadly snakes, but they need our protection.

Green anacondas might seem scary, but they are unlikely to hurt humans. These snakes live far from us—and we're not one of their favorite foods!

GLOSSARY

apex: the top or highest point of something

digest: to break down food inside the body so that the body can use it

endangered: in danger of dying out

fang: a long, pointed tooth

habitat: the natural place where an animal or plant lives

mate: one of two animals that come together to produce babies

nostril: an opening through which an animal breathes

shallow: not deep

strangle: to kill something by squeezing its throat

swamp: an area with trees that is covered with water at least part of the time

tropical: having to do with the warm parts of Earth near the equator

venom: something an animal makes in its body that can harm other animals.

vibration: a rapid movement back and forth

FOR MORE INFORMATION

Books

Boutland, Craig. *Green Anaconda*. Minneapolis, MN: Bearport Publishing Company, 2021.

Topacio, Francine. *Creatures in a Wet Rain Forest*. New York, NY: PowerKids Press, 2020.

Websites

Anaconda: Super Squeezers

kids.sandiegozoowildlifealliance.org/animals/anaconda
Discover more fun facts about anacondas at this website.

Green Anaconda

nationalzoo.si.edu/animals/green-anaconda
Find out more about one of the world's largest snakes here.

INDEX